MESHUGAH
A COMIC TRAGEDY

BY EMILY MANN

ADAPTED FROM THE NOVEL BY
ISAAC BASHEVIS SINGER

DRAMATISTS
PLAY SERVICE
INC.

MESHUGAH
Copyright © 2004, Emily Mann

All Rights Reserved

CAUTION: Professionals and amateurs are hereby warned that performance of MESHUGAH is subject to payment of a royalty. It is fully protected under the copyright laws of the United States of America, and of all countries covered by the International Copyright Union (including the Dominion of Canada and the rest of the British Commonwealth), and of all countries covered by the Pan-American Copyright Convention, the Universal Copyright Convention, the Berne Convention, and of all countries with which the United States has reciprocal copyright relations. All rights, including professional/amateur stage rights, motion picture, recitation, lecturing, public reading, radio broadcasting, television, video or sound recording, all other forms of mechanical or electronic reproduction, such as CD-ROM, CD-I, DVD, information storage and retrieval systems and photocopying, and the rights of translation into foreign languages, are strictly reserved. Particular emphasis is placed upon the matter of readings, permission for which must be secured from the Author's agent in writing.

The English language stock and amateur stage performance rights in the United States, its territories, possessions and Canada for MESHUGAH are controlled exclusively by DRAMATISTS PLAY SERVICE, INC., 440 Park Avenue South, New York, NY 10016. No professional or nonprofessional performance of the Play may be given without obtaining in advance the written permission of DRAMATISTS PLAY SERVICE, INC., and paying the requisite fee.

Inquiries concerning all other rights should be addressed to Creative Artists Agency, 162 Fifth Avenue, 6th Floor, New York, NY 10010. Attn: George Lane.

SPECIAL NOTE
Anyone receiving permission to produce MESHUGAH is required to give credit to the Author as sole and exclusive Author of the Play on the title page of all programs distributed in connection with performances of the Play and in all instances in which the title of the Play appears for purposes of advertising, publicizing or otherwise exploiting the Play and/or a production thereof. The names of the Author and Isaac Bashevis Singer must appear on separate lines, in which no other names appear, immediately beneath the title and in size of type equal to 50% of the size of the largest, most prominent letter used for the title of the Play. No person, firm or entity may receive credit larger or more prominent than that accorded the Author and Isaac Bashevis Singer. The billing must appear as follows:

MESHUGAH
A Comic Tragedy
by Emily Mann
adapted from the novel by Isaac Bashevis Singer

The following acknowledgment must appear on the title page in all programs distributed in connection with performances of the Play:

MESHUGAH was developed, in part, with the support of the Sundance Theatre Lab and originally produced by the McCarter Theatre Center, Princeton, NJ, Emily Mann, Artistic Director; Jeffrey Woodward, Managing Director.

*Inquire, I pray thee, of the former generation,
And apply thyself to that which their fathers have searched out —
For we are but of yesterday, and know nothing,
Because our days on earth are a shadow —
Shall not they teach thee, and tell thee,
And utter words out of their heart?*

—Job 8:8

AUTHOR'S NOTE

The play can be performed with five actors. Miriam, Max and Aaron do not double. The play must be staged without furniture being brought on and off.* The transitions are immediate and clean — seamless — often accomplished through light. The furniture is simple and minimal. Clothes, light and music tell the story. The play should be performed without a break.

* In the Boston production, there was a table and two chairs US, a bench SR, and a swivel office chair SL. These pieces transformed into all the locations.

DIRECTOR'S NOTE

What is forgivable?

Every value system is troubled by this question. Even asking it is problematic, for what gives us the right to forgive others? Who holds such moral authority? Yet however right or wrong, we do and do not forgive.

What if we encounter something that offends all that we value, something that we simply cannot forgive — and nevertheless we are asked to do so. For all our moral revulsion we cannot turn away but must find a way to accept. How can we? And what if we discover that we are looking at our own reflection? Where do we then find the strength to forgive ourselves?

Faced with these questions, we look for answers to some source of wisdom or guidance, either within ourselves, our family, our friends, our community, or our God. Humankind has struggled with these questions for thousands of years. Most of the time we find a way to cope, to survive, and to forgive. But what happens when all one knows — family, friends, community, and perhaps even God — is torn apart? The questions take on an entirely different meaning in a context of mass genocide.

Meshugah asks us to look full face at parts of ourselves that we would rather not see, parts that only come to light in the shadow of the Holocaust, when the unimaginable became real and every moral foundation was shaken or shattered. How do we make sense of a world that has turned crazy — meshugah?

On a personal note, it has been my honor and pleasure to work with Emily Mann. While her fearlessness as an artist has inspired me, I have been most touched by her generosity of spirit. It is BTW's great fortune that a major American playwright has entrusted her play to a small, relatively young theatre company. I, along with the entire organization, wish to thank Emily for the opportunity to nurture this work with her.

—Jason Slavick
Director for Meshugah
Boston Theatre Works

MESHUGAH premiered at the McCarter Theatre, in Princeton, New Jersey, on October 20, 1998. It was directed by Emily Mann; the set design was by Thomas Lynch; the lighting design was by Neil Peter Jampolis; the sound design was by David Budries; the original music was by Mel Marvin; the costume design was by Jennifer von Mayrhauser; the dramaturg was Janice Paran; and the production stage manager was Cheryl Mintz.** The cast was as follows:

AARON	David Chandler
MAX	Michael Constantine
WAITER	Jason Kolotouros
PRIVA	Rita Zohar
TZLOVA*	Gordana Rashovich
MIRIAM	Elizabeth Marvel
CHAIM JOEL*	Allen Swift
STANLEY	Jason Kolotrouros
LEON*	Allen Swift
STEFA*	Anne Scurria
MORRIS*	Allen Swift
WOMAN WHO TELLS	Rita Zohar
A RABBI*	Allen Swift

MESHUGAH was subsequently produced by Trinity Repertory Company (Oskar Eustis, Artistic Director; William P. Wingate, Managing Director) in Providence, Rhode Island, opening on February 25, 2000. It was directed by Oskar Eustis; the set design was by Michael McGarty; the lighting design was by D.M. Wood; the sound design was by Peter Hurowitz; the costume design was by William Lane; and the stage manager was Rosetta E. R. Lee. The cast was as follows:

AARON	Sam Tsoutsouvas
MAX	Tom Brennan
WAITER	Mauro Hantman
PRIVA	Barbara Orson
TZLOVA*	Anne Scurria
MIRIAM	Diana LaMar
JOEL TREIBITCHER*	Stephen Berenson
STANLEY BARDELES	Mauro Hantman

LEON*	Stephen Berenson
STEFA*	Anne Scurria
WOMAN WHO TELLS	Barbara Orson
MUSICIANS	Kevin Fallon
	Rachel Maloney, Chris Turner

A new version of MESHUGAH was workshopped at Boston Theatre Works (Jason Southerland, Artistic Director) in Boston, Massachusetts, opening on June 7, 2001. It was directed by Jason Slavick; the set design was by Susan Zeeman Rodgers; the lighting design was by Yael Lubetsky; the sound design was by Julie Pittman; the costume design was by Charlotte Burgess; and the stage manager was Julia Zayas-Melendez. The cast was as follows:

AARON	Ned Eisenberg
MAX	Ted Kazanoff
MIRIAM	Eileen Nugent
PRIVA, WOMAN WHO TELLS	Rena Baskin
STANLEY, WAITER	Jason Schuchman

MESHUGAH received its New York City premiere by Naked Angels (Tim Ransom, Artistic Director; Kourtney Keaton, Managing Director; Sherri Kotimsky, Producer) on May 7, 2003. It was directed by Loretta Greco; the set design was by Michael Brown; the lighting design was by James Vermeulen; the original music and sound design were by Rob Kaplowitz; the costume design was by Valerie Marcus; and the stage manager was Gillian Duncan. The cast was as follows:

AARON	Ned Eisenberg
MAX	Ben Hammer
MIRIAM	Elizabeth Marvel
PRIVA, WOMAN WHO TELLS	Barbara Andres
STANLEY, WAITER	Ted Koch

* Roles cut in final version.

** *Meshugah* was developed in part with the support of the Sundance Theatre Laboratory. The dramaturg was Shirley Fishman.

CHARACTERS

AARON GREIDINGER

MAX ABERDAM

MIRIAM ZALKIND

PRIVA

STANLEY BARDELES

WOMAN WHO TELLS

WAITER

PLACE

Manhattan's Upper West Side.

TIME

1952.

MESHUGAH

Music. Lights up. Aaron Greidinger enters The Jewish Daily Forward, *an isolated pool of light. He reads to himself from a sheaf of letters.*

AARON. "April 12, 1952. *The Jewish Daily Forward.* New York City. Dear Mr. Advisor, There is no one I can turn to who I can trust, only you. I think my wife of thirty-six years is going to leave me. I do not know English. I come from a village near Warsaw. I will be alone in this new country. My children were all killed in Stutthof. What should I do?" ... *(He picks up another letter.)* "Worthy Editor, Can you help me? My son no longer wants to be a Jew — as if this was possible ... He does not keep a kosher home, he has met a gentile girl ... " *(He picks up another letter.)* "Most Esteemed Advisor, I think I am dead. *(He stops for a moment.)* My lungs still breathe air, but I feel nothing." Ah, well. Of course, my friend. So do I. I, too, feel nothing. But what should you and I feel, huh? ... Our world no longer exists ... *(Picks up another letter. To the audience.)* What do I say to — the Communist who has become disillusioned with Stalin but seeks a new interpretation of Marxism; *(Another letter.)* the woman who has tried three times, since she survived the concentration camps, has tried three times to take her own life; *(Another letter.)* the young man who thinks that what has driven him to madness are "rays beamed at him by aliens"? Why have these people made up their minds that I alone can rescue them? *(He goes back to his work. Max Aberdam appears. Max, seventy, looks like he is still from the Jewish quarter in Warsaw — flowing tie, hat with a wide brim, he holds a cigar between his fingers, a gold watch chain hangs from his vest, gems sparkle from his cuff links.)*

MAX. Aaron Greidinger! Is it you? *(Aaron looks up, tries to hide his surprise.)* You look like you've seen a ghost. Don't be frightened, I haven't come from the Great Beyond to strangle you!
AARON. *(Shaken.)* Max? Max Aberdam? Can it be you?
MAX. Who else?
AARON. I thought you were killed in the camps years ago.
MAX. The Messiah has come and I arose from the dead. Hey ... Don't you read the news in your own newspaper? Or maybe you're the one who's dead? If that's the case, go back to your grave.
AARON. I'm alive ... I'm alive!
MAX. So have lunch with me, or I'll tear you apart like a herring.
AARON. *(Picking up the letters, shaken, covering.)* I'm sorry, I can hardly believe it ... But we have to make it another time ... My editors are waiting upstairs for these proofs.
MAX. So let them wait! This day belongs to me. The Jewish *Forward* will not fold up because you are out for half a day. Besides, you should quit the Jewish press. This is America! This is 1952! Why not write in English?
AARON. English? Who can express the lives of our people in English? If I am the last writer to write in Yiddish, I will write in Yiddish 'til the day I die.
MAX. *(Calming him down.)* All right, all right already. But what is this? *(Looks at pages.)* A story, I hope? A novel maybe? We are waiting for your next masterpiece, you know! *(He laughs.)* Or is this some more of your rotten advice?
AARON. Acch ... Some advice.
MAX. So, *nu,* so what's the rush then? *(Throwing the pages.)* This is beneath you. Why can't it wait 'til after lunch?
AARON. *(A big sigh, giving in.)* All right, all right already, it will wait 'til after lunch. *(Lights change. Max pulls Aaron to a table at Rappaport's restaurant. A surly waiter approaches them.)*
MAX. Coffee.
AARON. So, *nu?* So — Where have you been all during the war...?
MAX. Where have I been? Where have I not been! Bialystok, Vilna, Kovno, Shanghai, later in San Francisco. I have experienced the full range of Jewish woes. *(Aaron: "Yes ... ")* I left my wife and children behind in Warsaw in September of '39 — I thought I would send for them later — and like a lot of other people crossed the Praga Bridge towards Bialystok. Who knew it was already in Bolshevik hands ...

AARON. So what happened to you?
MAX. I was arrested, and was within a hairsbreadth of being stood against a wall and shot in the Lubyanka prison in Moscow when a Party functionary in the KGB — if you can believe it a former *accountant* of mine! — recognized me and saved me.
AARON. Incredible.
MAX. I fled east.
AARON. Where?
MAX. Shanghai. That the Jews are mad, this I've always known, but that they would be capable of founding a yeshiva in China where they quibble over the fate of an egg that was laid on a Sabbath as their families are being shoved into ovens in Europe — that I never imagined.
AARON. Nothing surprises me anymore.
MAX. No ... And your family?
AARON. All dead. And everyone I write about — all dead.
WAITER. Coffee.
AARON. And *your* family?
MAX. ... *(Pause.)* My wife and two daughters died in Stutthof. Aaron, don't dawdle, eat, eat! *(Takes a sip of coffee, nearly spits it out.)* Oy. *(To Aaron.)* In all America you cannot get a decent cup of coffee. *(Screams.)* Waiter! I ordered coffee, not dishwater. *(The waiter stomps over and takes away the coffee cup, muttering.)* So you never married or what?
AARON. No, I never married.
MAX. *(Wagging his finger at him.)* Of course. I know all about you, Aaron Greidinger. All the women at the Writer's Club in Warsaw talked about you.
AARON. What did they say?
MAX. Hah. What did they say? What did they not say? *(Laughs.)* You were a rascal! You could never stay away from the women at home. Nor they you ... Am I right? Everyone I used to meet and fall in love with talked about you. I would lie in bed with a beautiful woman and she would start to cry — "Aaron Greidinger has left me!"
AARON. Oh, stop, Max. It isn't true. It isn't true! *(Bitter, haunted.)* Anyway, all those women you and I loved — where are they now? I'm telling you, Max ... Some days it's hard to put one foot in front of the other.
MAX. *(With deep empathy.)* Of course it is ... So. Tell me ... it's been good for you here in America?
AARON. What can I say? We were lucky, my brother and I. And we

were dumb. Who knew? We came in the thirties; we missed the war.
MAX. ... Very lucky. Not so dumb.
AARON. ... So. Now my entire family is dead. Either they died in Europe, or they died here. My brother died just last year. *(Max mutters "I'm sorry.")* — A heart attack. I've written nothing of consequence since.
MAX. But that's nonsense! I know we Jews may not make our authors exactly rich — *(Aaron laughs.)* You look like a pauper —
AARON. I am a pauper ...
MAX. But *you are the finest writer we have*. Everyone agrees.
AARON. *(Agonized.)* No, no. Lately all I write is my advice column. Every day it's the same. I walk from my office at the newspaper to the Broadway Cafeteria, eat one meal a day, then travel home to my unheated room. I'm like a dead man. *(The waiter arrives with a new cup of coffee, slams it down.)*
WAITER. *(To Max.)* Coffee! Here!
MAX. All right.
WAITER. Enjoy it!
MAX. All right! *(The waiter leaves.)* But how can that be? So many of us are here! — from Lodz, from Warsaw! You have to see people, Aaron, meet people! I — for example — just found a distant relative, filthy rich, actually a millionaire, who fell upon me as if I were his long lost brother. He arranged a big loan for me, and now, I'm a stock market speculator.
AARON. ... Do you know anything about the stock market?
MAX. No, but who cares? I make money anyway! Look, lots of refugees here received a little reparation from Germany and have no idea what to do with it, especially the women. I've become their manager. I'm afraid that sooner or later I'll disappoint my crazy clients, but disappointing women has always been my trade. *(He eats and smokes.)*
AARON. Yes, I also disappoint women, I'm sorry to say.
MAX. Oh, thank God! I was afraid you might have become a prude, a preacher, or some other kind of American misfit. Seriously, though, Arale — I can't help myself. These women lost their husbands, their children ... They were driven half-mad in the ghettos and concentration camps. A human being has to love someone or he goes out like a candle. Don't you agree? *(Aaron nods, breaks away.)* And why deny it? I love them also. I am the kind of man who falls in love with every woman between twelve and eighty-nine.

AARON. *(Laughing.)* You stop at eighty-nine?
MAX. Not always. *(Aaron laughs. Max takes a sip of coffee.)* Uocch, this coffee is cold … *(He takes out a pill box, extracts two pills and takes them with the remaining coffee. He flinches with pain.)*
AARON. Max, what's wrong?
MAX. I'll tell you what's wrong. Everything the philosopher Oswald Spengler predicted after the First World War has come to pass after the Second. Whether it is social, or spiritual, or a result of God's madness, I don't know. I know only what my eyes see.
AARON. And what do your eyes see?
MAX. The world has turned *meshugah*. Come. There is someone I want you to meet. She's beautiful, intelligent, an absolute angel … What she has lived through she will tell you herself. But first, I'm afraid I have to introduce you to Priva, my present wife. She is always ill, and she is psychotic besides. She is my misfortune, but she is a faithful reader of yours. She told me more than once that if it were not for you and your scribblings, she would long ago have committed suicide and I would have become a widower, praise God. So you must go with me.
AARON. No, I couldn't possibly, Max. Really, I must return to my office.
MAX. No! You're not going back there today even if you stand on your head. I am here to bring you back to life! *(Music. Lights change. Out of the darkness, a woman with gray hair and a youthful face walks toward them. She wears a flowered robe and slippers with pompons. Diamonds sparkle in the lobes of her ears. Her narrow face, long neck, slender figure all radiate wealth and a kind of old Jewish nobility. When she sees Aaron, she makes a motion to retreat.)* Priva! *(Priva stops.)* Priva! Look who I've brought for you! Here is your great hero!
PRIVA. Oh, yes, I see!
MAX. This is Priva, my wife. *(Priva comes closer and stretches out a narrow hand.)*
PRIVA. It is an honor and a pleasure.
AARON. It is my pleasure.
PRIVA. I read what you write, every word, every week in the newspaper, under all your pseudonyms. But I have been waiting for a new story for months.
AARON. Oh, well. It's coming, it's coming …
PRIVA. Good. *(She flirts.)* You must promise me to stay for dinner.
AARON. Really, I cannot.
PRIVA. Why not? We'll cook the old Warsaw dishes for you.

Borscht, potato kugel, *kasha varnischkes* —
AARON. Unfortunately, I already have an engagement.
PRIVA. Well, I won't insist, even though I know you are lying to me.
AARON. No, no ... I am not.
PRIVA. But you must promise to come to us soon.
AARON. Yes, of course.
PRIVA. Tzlova, our maid, reads all your articles. When she wants to, she can prepare a meal fit for an emperor, and the Talmud says that the true emperors are those who are the learned — *(She looks at Max disparagingly.)* writers, men of the spirit. Excuse me. You must meet Tzlova! ... *(Priva hurries out. Max takes more pills.)*
MAX. So ... you see. I wanted a wife, and I got an institution.
AARON. How so? She is a fine woman! *(Max tries to cover his pain.)* Max, are you ill?
MAX. It's nothing, nothing! *(Referring to Priva.)* She's *too* fine. And not healthy. You can divorce a wife, but with an institution, you're stuck. She comes from a wealthy family of rabbis and merchants. As a child she knew the great writers Isaac Peretz, Herschl Nomberg, Hillel Zeitlin. They came to her home.
AARON. Ah. Fantastic.
MAX. No. She is a great *grande dame*. A snob. In San Francisco, when I met her, my mood was such that all I wanted was some rest. But all of a sudden, wild forces awoke in me. I walked into a trap from which there is no escape. *(Priva returns.)*
PRIVA. Tzlova won't come out! I begged her and begged her. She absolutely worships you, Mr. Greidinger. She listens to you on the radio every Sunday. She reads everything you write. And she is a darling. If it were not for her, I would have been among the dead long ago.
AARON. And why won't she come out?
PRIVA. She's cooking you dinner.
AARON. Ah! I see ... Bu —
PRIVA. You wrote recently that you long to have some Warsaw browned-flour soup. She'll make it for you better than you had it in Warsaw. At our house we had browned flour soup on Mondays and Thursdays.
AARON. As did we, as did we.
PRIVA. Tzlova is the best cook in existence. Whatever she cooks tastes as if it were made in Paradise. All you need is browned flour and fried onions. But — she adds a carrot, parsley and dill.
AARON. Well —

PRIVA. Mr. Greidinger, I stand by the window for hours and look out as they used to do in Poland in the old neighborhoods. I am looking for my friends. Where are they? ... In the Old Country, if you stood at the window for half an hour, *everyone* would pass by. But here in New York, to spot someone through a window is — how shall I say it — an anachronism.
AARON. Yes ... A whole world vanished forever.
MAX. Come, we have to go!
PRIVA. *(To Aaron.)* You're not staying for dinner? ... *(To Max.)* When will you be back? *(All three start speaking at once. To Aaron.)* When will we see you again?
MAX. I don't know. I have a hundred things to do. People are waiting for my checks. I mean, their checks.
PRIVA. *(Before Aaron can answer, to Max.)* Don't come back in the middle of the night. *(Max mutters, Priva turns to Aaron.)*
AARON. Soon, I'm sure
PRIVA. *(To Aaron.)* He wakes me up, and then I can't shut my eyes for the rest of the night. *(To Max.)* You fall asleep immediately but I lie and brood until daybreak. *Oy*, Mr. Greidinger ... what he puts me through! *(She extends her hand to Aaron.)* Another time perhaps?
AARON. Of course. A pleasure. *(As Aaron kisses her hand, lights change. Street noise.)*
MAX. *(Unsuccessfully hails a cab.)* TAXI! Aaron, I am in desperate straits about Miriam.
AARON. Miriam? Who is Miriam?
MAX. TAXI! Oh, to me, Miriam is still a child — a student! Young, pretty, intelligent ... I told you about her. But unfortunately, she married an American poet born in New York who is also young and a lunatic and now she is hoping to get a divorce.
AARON. Oh, I see.
MAX. *(As he pays.)* But I can't divorce Priva ... *(Aaron: "No ... ")* And what Miriam sees in me, I'll never know. She needs a young husband like you. *(Max and Aaron continue on.)* I could easily be her father, or her grandfather ...
AARON. Yes, yes.
MAX. Don't bray yes, yes like a DONKEY! Since you've become a dispenser of advice, maybe you can tell me how to manage this affair.
AARON. I can't even manage my own affairs. *(Music. Miriam stands before us. The men turn.)*
MAX. *Mein hartz ... mein neshuma ...* *(She has the face of a girl who seems no older than sixteen. Her dress is the dress of a Warsaw school-*

girl's, lacking the slightest pretense to elegance. no make-up, blazing eyes, she walks toward them, wraps herself around Max. He presents her with a small heart-shaped box of chocolates.)
MIRIAM. *(To Max.)* Chocolates again? Oh, I shall have to kill you!
MAX. Go ahead! Kill! This is New York. There'll be only one corpse more.
MIRIAM. *(Turns to Aaron.)* My name is Miriam.
AARON. *(Flushed, amazed by her.)* Aaron. Aaron Greidinger.
MIRIAM. *(Good-naturedly scolding Max.)* You didn't even introduce me! *(To Aaron.)* But I know who you are.
AARON. You do?
MIRIAM. I am Miriam, that's enough. *(She snatches the chocolates from Max, and they enter her apartment. The room is a bedroom with a large bed, unmade. She throws herself on it.)* I want you to know that I am your greatest fan in the whole world. I read every word you write.
MAX. Stop! He'll get a swelled head!
MIRIAM. I have written my dissertation about you.
AARON. No! That's impossible.
MIRIAM. You write the way people speak.
AARON. *(Smiling, pleased, almost embarrassed.)* Isn't that what a writer should do? ...
MIRIAM. Yes. But none of the others seem to do it.
AARON. Perhaps it's because I don't write fiction. *(Miriam howls.)*
MIRIAM. How do you mean you don't write fiction!
AARON. I make nothing up. I meet people, they tell me their lives, what happened to them, especially during the war, and I write it down. It's simple.
MIRIAM. *(Suddenly old.)* It isn't simple. A whole world collapsed before my very eyes. But you, my favorite author, you bring it back to life.
AARON. No. No writer can possibly resurrect what the wicked have destroyed.
MIRIAM. *(Revealed.)* Yes ... I know ... *(They stare at each other.)*
MAX. Love at first sight, huh? ... Hey! — when I bring a guest to meet my girl, I want her to receive him properly. Put on some shoes, serve some food. I'll help you clean up. This is an apartment, not a pigsty, you wild creature. *(He playfully slaps her behind. She laughs.)*
MIRIAM. And what are you? You didn't even give me a kiss. *(As he takes her in his arms:)*
MAX. You don't deserve a kiss. *(She gives Aaron a flirtatious look as she and Max kiss. Aaron turns away.)*

MIRIAM. Sit, Mr. Greidinger. I've made coffee. *(She leaves to get the coffee. As Max straightens the bed proprietarily, Aaron straightens his tie, his hair. From off.)* Mr. Greidinger —
AARON. *(Calling To her.)* Please, Aaron!
MIRIAM. *"Aaron"* — the other day I read a piece of yours about a religion of protest. What did you mean by it? Don't laugh, but "someone" *(Looking at Max as she enters with coffee.)* had torn out a part of the page, and I was unable to finish it. *(They laugh.)*
MAX. He probably forgot what he meant. He has a dozen pseudonyms, and he has to deliver copy constantly. He writes whatever comes into his head.
MIRIAM. *(Sitting with Max.)* Oh, hush, Maxele. Let him answer.
AARON. No, I certainly did not forget. What I meant was that one may believe in God's wisdom and yet deny that He is the source of goodness only. God and mercy are not absolutely synonymous.
MAX. How is protest going to help us?
AARON. We will no longer be flatterers and masochists. We will no longer kiss the rod that whips us.
MAX. I don't know about you, but I am quite willing to do without God and the whole religious paraphernalia that goes with him.
AARON. On what would you base ethics?
MAX. There is no base and no ethics.
AARON. In other words, might is right?
MAX. So it seems.
MIRIAM. Oh, Max …
AARON. If might is right, Hitler was right.
MAX. Inasmuch as he was defeated, he was not right. If he had won, all the nations of the world would have joined hands with him. The entire world.
MIRIAM. Really. Max, you are wrong. We Jews must never entertain the notion that there is no morality in the universe and that man may do whatever he likes.
MAX. And what does Jewishness consist of? When we Jews had might, four thousand years ago, we fell upon the Canaanites, the Girgashim, the Prizim, and we wiped them out, every man, woman, and child. What, Aaron Greidinger, is your definition of God?
AARON. The plan behind evolution, the Power which moves the galaxies …
MAX. That power is blind and knows no plan. There is nothing but chaos.
MIRIAM. Yet, you're always speaking of God, Max. You even fast

on Yom Kippur.

MAX. Not from piety. I do it in remembrance of my parents. One can be a Jew without believing in God.

MIRIAM. Well, yes, that is certainly true for me. *(Aaron looks at her. She looks back. Max, seeing this:)*

MAX. Excuse me, my children. I have to telephone someone by nine o'clock. Business calls. *(Max goes off into the other room. He can be heard off, picking up the phone and doing business. Aaron puts down his coffee cup.)*

MIRIAM. I still can scarcely believe that you are here in my apartment. Being together with you and Max makes me feel as if I were still in Warsaw and what came later was only a nightmare.

AARON. What happened to you? Do you mind my asking?

MAX. *(Off.)* Stocks? Which stocks? I told you to sell those stocks!

MIRIAM. If I were granted one wish before I die ... I would ask that you and Max move in with me, so that we three could be together.

AARON. You are too young to be speaking of death.

MIRIAM. Too young? I have stared death in the face for years.

AARON. Ah ... I see ...

MIRIAM. Aaron? *(Miriam runs up to Aaron and kisses him passionately.)*

MAX. *(Off.)* Texaco? How much? Wait, Hershele, I will write it down. Hershele, wait —

AARON. *(Trying to cover, smooth over what has just happened; shaken and aroused.)* Who, uh ... who is Hershele?

MIRIAM. *(Laughing.)* His name is Harry Treibitcher, not Hershele; he's American-born. Max insists on calling him Hershele. He is a speculator, an adventurer, he plays the horses. But Max has given him "power of attorney"— and that is sheer madness! — By the way, how do you say "power of attorney" in Yiddish?

AARON. In Yiddish, there is no such word. In my father's court, "power of permission" was used. He was a rabbi.

MIRIAM. Yes, I know. There were rabbis in my family, too. Also Hasidim. *(They stare at each other.)* During the war, when I was in hiding, I read Dostoevsky in French and found him absolutely entrancing. You are like a character from Dostoevsky. You always keep yourself hidden. In my unfinished dissertation I call you "the Hider." You know, I've given my life a goal — to make you famous. *(He laughs.)* Don't laugh. Someone has to do it.

AARON. But I am dissatisfied with my creative work. Perhaps

your life's goal is empty.

MIRIAM. I don't think so. *(She leans back on the bed.)* You know, I have another ambition — actually two.

AARON. *(Flustered, amazed.)* ... What are they?

MIRIAM. To tell you all that I have lived through — everything, leaving out nothing, not even the most foolish things. *(Aaron looks at her, heart in mouth.)*

AARON. What is the second ambition?

MIRIAM. That one I'd better not mention today. *(She laughs. They stare at each other. Max enters, practically dancing.)*

MAX. The market is going up! We are reaping shovelfuls of gold in the land of Columbus. And what are you two doing? She probably told you every possible evil about me. Don't believe a word of it. She takes after you, a born storyteller. Listen children, I've just learned that I must travel to Poland.

MIRIAM. To Poland?!

MAX. My father left me a house in Lodz, and the Poles are finally letting me sell it — for one-tenth of its value, naturally.

MIRIAM. *(Frightened.)* When are you leaving?

MAX. Soon. If the whole affair is a trap and the Communists are bent on liquidating me, you two will know what to do.

MIRIAM. *(Angry, through tears.)* How can you go back to Poland? Poland is a graveyard. *(She looks to Aaron for understanding.)* Aaron, *tell* him! *(To Max.)* You must be drunk.

MAX. I was born drunk. Pif-paf! A world full of wonders. *(Wipes away her tears.)* Listen, my darling, what became of our supper, huh? *(Miriam looks at Aaron, frightened. Max puts his arm around her and moves her away. Music. Lights change. Aaron alone. A surreal light. Sounds.)*

AARON. That night, I dreamt I'm back in Poland with my family ... and all the other lost souls. I'm scrambling over mass graves Jews dug for themselves. The mounds of earth are moving and muffled cries rise from below, cries for help; those still alive are trying to crawl out from under the corpses smothering them. I'm one of those struggling for life. *(The phone rings. lights change. Aaron picks up the phone.)* Yes?

MIRIAM. *(Off.)* May I speak with Mr. Greidinger?

AARON. Speaking. *(A Pause.)*

MIRIAM. *(Off.)* I hope I didn't wake you. This is Miriam, remember me?

AARON. *(Formal, covering his delight.)* You didn't wake me. Yes, Miriam. It's ... very good to hear from you.

MIRIAM. *(Off.)* Ah … *(Pause. Laughs.)* I told you last evening of the dissertation I am writing about you. It occurred to me that you might meet with me before I went to work. Perhaps Max told you I'm a baby-sitter.
AARON. No, he did not.
MIRIAM. *(Off.)* Yes. For a little boy named Didi. He's a darling. They live on Park Avenue. By the way, how do you say "baby-sitter" in Yiddish?
AARON. There is no such idea.
MIRIAM. I have a great many questions to ask you. I know it is presumptuous, and if you have no time or patience for me today, I won't feel insulted.
AARON. I have both time and patience.
MIRIAM. *(Off.)* Have you had breakfast?
AARON. No, I was on my way to the Broadway Cafeteria.
MIRIAM. *(Off.)* May I join you?
AARON. Yes, yes. Of course.
MIRIAM. *(Off.)* Good. By the time you reach the cafeteria I'll be there.
AARON. Where is Max?
MIRIAM. *(Off.)* Max and I spoke about you for a long time last night. That I love you is not altogether astonishing *(Aaron is stunned.)*, but Max said last night that you are like a son to him. Ah, I have so much to tell you, and I don't even know where to begin. Bye! *(She hangs up. Aaron, amazed, hangs up. ("Bye … ") Lights change and Miriam enters, resplendent in white. Aaron's heart pounds. He walks toward her. Miriam takes Aaron's arm, and they enter the cafeteria. Aaron sees an empty table by a window and grabs it.*
AARON. Sit, sit. I'll get us food.
MIRIAM. I'm not really hungry. I want nothing more than coffee. *(Aaron nods. They are both breathless, looking at each other. He goes to get food. She watches him. The cafeteria is full of refugees. One hears only Yiddish and some Polish. Aaron gets breakfast for both of them and returns.)*
AARON. Whatever is here is for you.
MIRIAM. But I've eaten. *(She tastes the fruit and grabs a roll. She laughs.)* Mmmmm. Good. *(They both eat. Miriam is hunched over her food, eats voraciously. Aaron sees what she has been through.)*
AARON. We sit here. We're two refugees. But it is you who's Hitler's victim, not me. You have faced countless perils until you found a haven in this blessed land, where a Jewish girl can study at a univer-

sity, rent an apartment, even write a dissertation on an unknown Yiddish writer. *(She presses her knee against his leg under the table.)*
MIRIAM. You know I am not a moralist.
AARON. Good.
MIRIAM. I have had men in Poland as well as here, and I always had the illusion that I loved each man, or at least that he loved me. At the same time that I study, read, become inspired by you and others — dream of happiness, of having a child — I become tired of this cursed game and want to put an end to it.
AARON. No, no. Don't say it.
MIRIAM. Have you noticed how many refugees from the camps wait to kill themselves here in America?
AARON. Yes, there is such a thing as feeling you did not deserve to live.
MIRIAM. Yes. In Max, this feeling is even stronger than in me.
AARON. Really?
MIRIAM. He wants to provide for everyone, all the refugees, but especially for me. You know his wife and two children died — *(Hard to say.)* in Stutthoff.
AARON. Yes.
MIRIAM. *(Taking his hand.)* And you? Do you ever feel you did not deserve to live?
AARON. All the time.
MIRIAM. Good.
AARON. Good?
MIRIAM. Yes, good. I understand you. *(Releasing his hand, turning away.)* Max probably told you that I have a husband.
AARON. Yes.
MIRIAM. Stanley Bardeles. He's a maniac, a compulsive scribbler without talent. He refuses to grant me a divorce and creates all sorts of difficulties. Max has convinced himself that I am a helpless little girl, a child, but in fact I often have the feeling that I am old, very old.
AARON. How many men have you had? *(Aaron looks down, immediately regretting his lack of tact.)*
MIRIAM. *(Smiling.)* Why do you ask?
AARON. Ah. I don't know. Foolish curiosity.
MIRIAM. I had many.
AARON. Twenty?
MIRIAM. At least.
AARON. Why did you do it?
MIRIAM. When you are lying in a hole for many months, a hole

so small you can barely stretch your legs — and your life is threatened — every encounter with someone from the world of the living is an exciting event.

AARON. What is this hole you were lying in for many months?

MIRIAM. When our apartment was seized, my mother was sent to a concentration camp and I was smuggled out of the ghetto to the Aryan side. I was fifteen. A former teacher of mine hid me in a dark alcove where old furniture was stored. I was forced to pay the concierge's son bribe money to let me stay. He also forced me to submit to him, and when he came to me he held a knife to my throat.

AARON. I'm sorry.

MIRIAM. When I finally came out to freedom and saw a city of ruins, I felt as if through some miracle I had risen from my grave. You wrote a story like this —

AARON. "In the World of Chaos." Its hero is a corpse who doesn't know that he is dead.

MIRIAM. Yes ... it was my life ... Sometimes, hiding in barns, or fields, I would sleep near a man who, without a word, would climb on me. There was no sense creating a scandal. Agents from Palestine, members of the *Brikha* came to help us. These "rescuers" were also men, not angels ...

AARON. I see ...

MIRIAM. I am sure that you find me repulsive, now that I've told you these things. But since you asked, I wanted to answer.

AARON. I had no right to ask. And it is the murderers I find repulsive, not the victims.

MIRIAM. What does a woman have in such circumstances? Nothing but her body. *(Aaron: "Ah ... ")* When we reached Germany we were placed in a camp again —

AARON. Again? What do you mean, another camp?

MIRIAM. No, no. We were placed in a kind of camp, I mean, a refugee camp, not a concentration camp — to await our visas for America or Palestine. So ... we were still ... inmates ... of a camp. *(Miriam is overwhelmed. She looks at her watch.)* Oh, my God, it's a quarter to eleven. I must get to my babysitting job on Park Avenue!

AARON. May I walk you?

MIRIAM. Of course. Every minute with you is pure joy for me.

AARON. Why do you say that?

MIRIAM. The other day Max asked me whom I would like as my future husband or lover — and I answered immediately, Aaron Greidinger. Max wants to provide me with a husband. I hope you

don't mind, but Max is older than you are. He must be my number one until he dies. Do you mind being number two?
AARON. *(Barely able to talk.)* I would be delighted.
MIRIAM. Are you serious?
AARON. Completely. *(Lights change. Music.* The Jewish Daily Forward. *Aaron writes his advice column. Max enters, popping pills.)*
MAX. Aaron Greidinger!
AARON. *(Looks up.)* Max? ... What are you doing here?
MAX. Call Miriam immediately. You two are coming to a party with me tonight.
AARON. What? I — I couldn't possibly.
MAX. What are you talking about?
AARON. I don't like parties. I don't like crowds of people.
MAX. Don't give me that nonsense. You're coming. It's not a crowd. You are invited to Chaim Joel Treibitcher's house, for dinner.
AARON. Who?
MAX. Chaim Joel is a philanthropist for Jewish arts. He's rich, he'll back you. You'll come. With Miriam.
AARON. Max ... no, really ...
MAX. Call Miriam. *(He squeezes Aaron's cheeks.)* She has the address, dahlink. See you tonight! CALL MIRIAM NOW! *(He exits. Aaron sighs, thinks, calls Miriam. Lights change.)*
MIRIAM. Hello.
AARON. Miriam? It's me. Aaron.
MIRIAM. Ah ... I know ... I recognized your voice immediately. *(Pause.)*
AARON. Ah ...
MIRIAM. I just finished work ...
AARON. Yes ... *(Long pause.)* Your babysitting ...
MIRIAM. Yes ...
AARON. You know, Max just came by inviting us to a party.
MIRIAM. Yes. I know. Max insists I take you or you will remain impoverished, a *shnorrer* forever. *(They laugh.)* You know this Chaim Joel? *(Aaron: "No ... ")* He is an absolute angel and his nephew Harry is a complete and total scoundrel. I told you about Harry, remember ...
AARON. Yes ...
MIRIAM. The first night we met.
AARON. Yes ...
MIRIAM. You know Max asked me to go with him to Poland, but the thought of being there again, of walking amongst the dead,

makes me shudder. *(Lights reveal Miriam is half-clothed on her bed.)*
AARON. I understand.
MIRIAM. What are you doing right now? *(Aaron looks at his work.)*
AARON. Ah, nothing at all.
MIRIAM. Come over.
AARON. What? ... When?
MIRIAM. Now. This minute.
AARON. I — I —
MIRIAM. I need you. I need you now.
AARON. *(Long pause.)* I need you, too. *(Music. Miriam slowly slips off her dressing gown. She is in a flimsy slip. In the light she looks almost naked. Aaron turns ... They see each other, move together. They embrace without a word. Lights change as they start to make love, passionately. Blackout. Lights come up. Aaron and Miriam are still in bed but it is now twilight, not afternoon. They are asleep. Miriam stirs. Half-asleep she whispers:)*
MIRIAM. Max? *(Aaron stirs.)*
AARON. No, it's me.
MIRIAM. *(Murmuring.)* Come. Butterfly. I think I shall call you Butterfly.
AARON. I want nothing but to be with you. *(They embrace.)* Until now, I never believed I could love a woman knowing that she loved another. *(Miriam laughs.)*
MIRIAM. Is that true?
AARON. Well, in truth, I realize it has happened before. I have loved women who had husbands.
MIRIAM. Of course.
AARON. And I took great pains to tell these women that their husbands should be number one.
MIRIAM. I should hope so.
AARON. It is pleasant to know that I need not demand of my beloved what I am not prepared to ask of myself.
MIRIAM. I want to know everything about you — about who you've loved, about all your women — who has loved you back ...
AARON. Ahhhh ...
MIRIAM. The last one, the last love — did she break your heart? *(A pause.)*
AARON. No, the truth is, sadly, I have never loved a woman I couldn't leave. *(She pulls him to her. They kiss.)*
MIRIAM. I know you, I have studied every word you have written. I have loved you for so long ... Would you like to know everything

about *me?*

AARON. I would like nothing more ... No one can ever kiss me or attract me or satisfy me as you have. We have already loved how many times before in how many other lifetimes. We were fish in the sea together, *(Miriam: "Yes.")* we were birds in the air. We two were in the garden of Eden; I was Adam and you were Eve, and when you had me taste the forbidden fruit, we were cast out of Paradise together. Together we were slaves in the land of Egypt. We were forty days and forty nights in the desert, and when the moment of liberation came, we entered the land of milk and honey, and I could never get enough of your milk, your honey ... *(She laughs.)*

MIRIAM. God toys with us, Aaron Greidinger ... *(They start to make love. Soon we hear a fumbling at the front door; Miriam jerks away with a scream. Aaron bolts up. Suddenly the hall ceiling light is on. Silhouetted, is a young man, short and stocky with long hair and a black beard, dressed in a pink shirt, dirty trousers, holding a revolver. Miriam has snuck up on the man, ready to strike, but stops.)* Stanley!

STANLEY. Yes, it's me.

MIRIAM. What do you want?

STANLEY. You.

MIRIAM. You see that I have someone.

STANLEY. *(Pointing the revolver at Aaron.)* Hey, you. If you want to live a few years longer, better get out of here. Otherwise they'll carry you out.

AARON. May I get dressed?

STANLEY. Yeah. Take your rags and go into the bathroom. Make no attempt to get help or I'll —

AARON. Just a moment. *(Aaron draws a cover around him. his feet touch the floor and almost buckle.)*

STANLEY. Wait a minute. I know you, I know you. You're the writer, Aaron Greidinger. I'm a writer, too.

AARON. Yes, yes. Mr. Stanley, I am acquainted with your situation — I know you are her husband — and I can understand your feeling, but there is no need to point a gun at us. We are putting up no resistance.

MIRIAM. Stanley, don't make a fool of yourself. Put down the revolver.

STANLEY. I've come to put an end either to your stinking life or to mine. I won't kill this man, but you, you filthy whore, soon you'll be dead and gone. Mr. Greidinger, I think you should know that you have been consorting with a whore. She was a whore at fifteen; she told me so herself. In 1939, when her parents left for Russia, she refused to join them because she was the mistress of a pimp. Later he brought her over to the Aryan side and put her in a brothel. Is this true or not?

MIRIAM. It's not true.

STANLEY. You told me so yourself with your own filthy mouth. Nazis were your clients. They brought you gifts they seized from murdered Jewish girls. Am I lying? Answer me, or this will be your last moment.

MIRIAM. I didn't want to die at sixteen.

STANLEY. You could have crossed the bridge with your parents, instead of taking up with a pimp. Am I telling the truth?

MIRIAM. At sixteen, I wanted to live. Now I no longer do. You can shoot me this instant, you psychopath!

AARON. Miriam, this cannot be true. *(She does not answer.)*

STANLEY. *(To Aaron.)* Go use the bathroom, and make it quick. *(Aaron gropes for the door, feeling weak.)*

AARON. *(Weakly, feeling foolish.)* Excuse me. *(He goes into the bathroom. he starts to dress, feels faint, nearly swoons, gets sick in the sink. Stanley advances on Miriam, tries to kiss her. She fights him off. Stanley screams at Aaron through the door.)*

STANLEY. It's all true! You're a writer, a son of a rabbi! You should know what you are and who you've taken up with.

MIRIAM. *(In a hiss.)* He already knows everything.

STANLEY. How could he know everything? Even I don't know everything. Whenever I meet someone who knows you, I learn of more lovers, more affairs, more lies.

MIRIAM. I told you the truth right from the beginning. *(Aaron emerges from the bathroom, white, ill, wearing pants and shirt.)*

STANLEY. Put on your tie. Before you go, I want to ask you a question. Is it true that you believe in God?

AARON. I believe in His wisdom, not in His mercy.

STANLEY. I would like to speak with you someday about this, but not now.

MIRIAM. Aaron … *(He looks at her.)*

STANLEY. Go. If you read in the papers that we're both dead, you'll know why.

AARON. Don't do it. If she is as you say, she is not worth dying for.

MIRIAM. And what is worth dying for? *(Aaron looks at her a long time, then walks past them.)*

STANLEY. *(Calling after him.)* If you call the police, I'll kill both of us immediately.

MIRIAM. Aaron?! *(Aaron will not look at Miriam. He stumbles out. falls. Stanley drags Miriam off. Aaron sits on a park bench. rocks. holds his head.)*

AARON. No, no, no ... Miriam ... *He rocks, recites a prayer for the dead. He holds his head. Surreal light. Music. Passage of time to early morning. Exhausted, spent, he goes to his office at the* Jewish Forward. *A phone is ringing. He hears it, stares at it. It stops. He throws himself into his chair, frightened, angry. It rings again. It keeps ringing. He tries to defy it but finally, exhausted, he answers. Long pause.)* Yes?

MIRIAM. It's me, the whore. *(Aaron makes a motion to hang up the phone, but he clings to it.)* You left your keys in my apartment, also your checkbook and some money. Like Tamar, the whore, I want to return thy signet, thy bracelet, and thy staff.

AARON. Tamar pretended to be a prostitute, but you *are* one.

MIRIAM. Then how is it that a man as saintly as Judah went to her?

AARON. Miriam, this is not the time to discuss tales from the Pentateuch.

MIRIAM. When is the proper time? I want to give you your things. I may be a whore but I am not a thief.

AARON. Miriam, everything is finished between us.

MIRIAM. I want to return your property. *(He struggles.)*

AARON. Meet me at the cafeteria.

MIRIAM. Good. *(Aaron slowly hangs up the phone. Music starts. He turns, drawn to the sound. Out of the darkness, Miriam appears. She wears a red dress and red boots. From her scarlet lips, a cigarette dangles. Aaron sees her and loses his breath. The street noise is deafening.)*

AARON. No ... *(She walks slowly downstage. He approaches her, enraged. In strangled voice.)* You planned it all. The quote from the Pentateuch, that Warsaw whore's getup you're sporting. I should be arrested. *(She laughs.)* You've made fools of me, Max, Stanley, and the devil knows who else ...

MIRIAM. You said you wanted to know everything about me. Well, this is what I was and what I shall always be. I don't feel guilty, not for a minute. It was foolish at sixteen to fall in love with a scoundrel like Yanek and to endure all I have endured. But what is the sense of feeling remorse? Repentance is a religious concept. If one does not believe in a personal God or in sexual morality, how can there be any repentance for what I have done? *I wanted to live.* I was prepared to die, and the fact that I survived at least physically is something I cannot explain. If I have any regrets, it is that I kept the truth from you and Max. But the truth surfaced anyway, as they say — like oil on water.

AARON. A person like you should not even breathe the word "truth."

MIRIAM. ... Maybe so ... But it is still a fact that I have lived, suffered, and hoped. You once quoted Spinoza in one of your stories. "There are no lies, only distorted truths." Even a worm has its own small truth. It is born, it lives briefly, then it is trampled under someone's foot. Those are your words, not mine. *(She smiles.)*

AARON. What happened after I left?

MIRIAM. You want to know.

AARON. You are not obliged to answer. *(Pause.)*

MIRIAM. Things happened. Stanley stayed with me the whole night. I did not expect to live 'til morning, and I was prepared to die. Stanley was not the first to threaten me with a revolver. That same Yanek for whom I had sacrificed my life amused himself by shooting a glass tumbler which he put on my head. He brought his colleagues — Poles, not Germans — and they played the same game. This is but one of hundreds of true stories, whether you believe them or not. Don't think that I have come to you to cry or to apologize. I owe you nothing. Not you, not even Max.

AARON. Where is Max?

MIRIAM. Max is on his way to Poland.

AARON. Did you see him before he left?

MIRIAM. How could I? The telephone rang, but Stanley forbade me to pick it up. I found out that this morning, after the party, Max left for Poland together with Matilda Treibitcher, Chaim Joel's wife.

AARON. How did you get rid of your husband?

MIRIAM. My husband, huh? *(She laughs.)* Since he didn't kill me, sooner or later he had to be on his way. Before he left, he said that he was ready to divorce me. It was funny, really funny.

AARON. Why was it funny?

MIRIAM. He couldn't decide whether to kill me or not. He kept talking about it, and finally he asked my advice. Have you ever heard such a thing? In the midst of my so-called tragedy, I had to laugh.

AARON. What was your advice?

MIRIAM. My advice was: Do what you like.

AARON. Is this one of your distorted truths?

MIRIAM. ... This is what happened.

AARON. And then?

MIRIAM. He said good-bye and left. One minute he spoke about killing me and the next, he babbled about a reconciliation. He even proposed that we have a child together. I would not have believed it to be possible, except after what I have seen in my life, nothing about the human race can shock me anymore. You may be a writer, but I know more of what human beings are capable of than you.

AARON. What about the teacher and the dark alcove in which you allegedly spent the war years — was that also a lie?

MIRIAM. It was not a lie. I didn't struggle hard to stay alive — what for? But a sort of ambition grew in me to overcome everything and to come through those swinish times alive and strong. I would say it became a sort of gamble or sport for me: Will I make it or will I not? The day it became clear to me that I would be grabbed and sent away with one of the transports, I fled from Yanek, and my former teacher took me in.

AARON. When was that?

MIRIAM. The end of 1942. No, it was already 1943.

AARON. Did your teacher know of your conduct?

MIRIAM. Yes; no. Who knows?

AARON. And it was at her house that you read all those books?

MIRIAM. *(Uncomfortable.)* Yes, at her house.

AARON. And then?

MIRIAM. In 1945, I crawled out, like a mouse from a hole, and another chapter began — wandering, sneaking across borders, sleeping in barns, in ditches, and all the rest.

AARON. What happened to your pimp?

MIRIAM. Someone gave him his due. *(They sit a long time. Miriam makes a motion to open her bag.)* Look, I have your property. Your money, keys, checkbook.

AARON. Please. Not here in the street.

MIRIAM. Where did Tamar return Judah's belongings? *(Aaron looks at her, cold, stung. Angry.)* None of you has the right to point a finger at me. Not you, not Max, not that idiot Stanley. How am I a whore any more than you are a lecher? What do you think goes on in middle-class America, or for that matter, in the Jewish State? What of the women in America whose husbands lavish furs and jewelry and Cadillacs on them while they themselves while away their time with all sorts of trash? How am I worse than the girls in my college? Heaven knows how many men my classmates have had. At least I was trying to rescue my stinking life. Most of the Jewish girls who fell into Nazi hands would have done the same if they had been given half the chance. *(They sit a long time without speaking.)*

Here is your property. *(Miriam opens her handbag and hands Aaron the keys, checkbook and the dollars he had in an envelope.)* You can tell Max everything that happened. Just remember that I can manage without men, too. If you like, this can be our last meeting. *(Long pause.)* Look at the sky! *(Long pause.)*
AARON. Beautiful.
MIRIAM. Butterfly — I can no longer live without you. That's the bitter truth.
AARON. Huh ... the bitter truth ... *(?)* So soon?
MIRIAM. With me everything happens quickly. Either quickly or not at all.
AARON. What about Max?
MIRIAM. I miss him, too.
AARON. And Stanley?
MIRIAM. *(Shivers.)* Don't mention his name, may it be cursed. Butterfly, I have an idea. But promise not to laugh at it.
AARON. I will not laugh.
MIRIAM. Since you already know the truth about me, let everything remain as it is.
AARON. Let what remain as it is?
MIRIAM. I will be a prostitute and you will be my client. My apartment will be our brothel. You will pay me — but I will be cheap. A dollar a week, or ten cents a night. There were cheap prostitutes in Warsaw, in fact on your street.
AARON. What about Max?
MIRIAM. He will call me that too. I no longer want to play deceptive games. I want to be an honest prostitute. *(Aaron almost wants to laugh, but he also feels a stinging in his eyes.)*
AARON. And what of the others?
MIRIAM. What others? There will be no others.
AARON. A prostitute with two clients only?
MIRIAM. Yes, you and Max. If Max does not want me, I'll be yours alone. *(A long pause.)*
AARON. What shall we do now?
MIRIAM. Give me ten cents.
AARON. In advance?
MIRIAM. In Warsaw, they always paid in advance.
AARON. Wait. *(Aaron digs in his trouser pocket until he finds a dime. Miriam stretches out her hand.)* Here. *(He puts the dime in her hand. Miriam holds the coin for a while and stares at it. then she takes it with her other hand and holds the dime to her lips.)*

MIRIAM. This is the happiest night of my life. *(Tears stream down her face. Slow fade to black. Music. A lullaby. Lights up on Miriam's apartment, weeks later. Aaron lies on the bed, writing, making notes. Miriam sings the lullaby to the baby, Didi, off.)*
AARON. What are you singing?
MIRIAM. *(Calling.)* An old lullaby. Do you know it?
AARON. *(Calling to her, off.)* I don't know ... *(She sings. He listens, remembers.)* Yes ... I'm surprised to say I do. *(He goes back to his writing, then looks up.)* Just remember he isn't yours. You have to give him back!
MIRIAM. I know, I know ... *(She laughs, enters with the baby. Sits on the bed with Aaron.)* I wish we would hear from Max ...
AARON. I phoned Chaim Joel again today. I have phoned repeatedly — all week. No one is at home.
MIRIAM. *(Suddenly cold.)* Do you think they have arrested Max in Poland?
AARON. *(Not sure himself.)* Of course they haven't. Why would they?
MIRIAM. Who knows what they are capable of doing to us there. *(She stares at the baby. Miriam suddenly laughs.)*
AARON. What?
MIRIAM. Look, Arale, isn't the baby a darling?
AARON. For the time being.
MIRIAM. What do you mean by that?
AARON. He'll probably grow up to be a thief, a crook, or a murderer.
MIRIAM. How can you say that? It is more likely he'll become an honest man, an artist, a scholar. Like you. *(She looks at Aaron.)* Take him.
AARON. What? I don't know how to hold a baby.
MIRIAM. Take him. Like this. He's almost asleep. *(She gives him the baby. He holds him awkwardly, then more comfortably. She starts to sing the old Yiddish lullaby. He is surprised he knows the rest of it. As he sings, he gets more and more engrossed with the baby. Miriam exits, leaving him alone with the baby.)*
AARON. You know, I've never wanted a child; I never wanted to bring a new soul into this accursed world, but tonight — I feel such tenderness ... for you ... you, who are entirely helpless, you who are entirely dependent on our kindness. *(Miriam comes in, frantic, with a copy of the Jewish* Forward.*)*
MIRIAM. Arale, Arale! Oh, my God, my punishment has come

at last. He's lost *everything*. Everybody's money!
AARON. What? *(She reads him the headline.)*
MIRIAM. "Max Aberdam, who speculated with the money of Polish refugees — " *(She stops.)*
AARON. No, no ... It can't be!
MIRIAM. Max's heart will break. Oh, my God, my God ... I warned Max, I told him. The very first time I met you I told you that Harry was a swindler and a gambler. Oh, Aaron, this was not simply money. This was gut money, blood money, reparation money refugee mothers received for their children ... *(Miriam breaks down.)* ... This will be what finally kills him ... What does God want, Aaron? He must want something ... *(She exits with the baby. Aaron looks after her, helpless. The phone rings.)*
AARON. Yes?
MAX. *(V. O.)* I've returned from my grave to strangle you. *(His heart leaps.)*
AARON. Where are you? Where are you calling from? *(Calling off.)* MIRIAM! *(No answer.)*
MAX. I am in New York. I just flew from Europe. Arale, I am here incognito. Even Priva doesn't know I've arrived. If my refugees find out I'm here, they'll tear me limb from limb, and they have a right to do so.
AARON. Why didn't you write to us? *(Calling off.)* MIRIAM! We sent you cables. To Poland, to Matilda's house in Switzerland ...
MAX. All the curses of the Holy Book rained down on my head during this trip.
AARON. Where are you now?
MAX. In the Empire Hotel on Broadway. How is Miriam?
AARON. She's worried sick about you ... She must have just gone out.
MAX. Listen, Arale — I became seriously ill in Poland. Miriam was right. Poland is a graveyard. Matilda went back to her childhood village. She suffered a heart attack there. She's dead.
AARON. What ...
MAX. She's lucky. After many difficulties, Chaim Joel managed to take her body to Eretz Yisrael. She will lie there with other righteous men and women. As for me, it seems that I'll have to make do with a grave in New York.
AARON. What do you mean? What are you planning to do?
MAX. I don't know. I was given the name of an American doctor, a world authority in the field. I cabled him but have received no

answer. I don't want to die among strangers.

AARON. I'll come right over.

MAX. No, no. Come over tomorrow, quietly. No one must know I am here. *(Miriam appears, looks at Aaron and knows he is talking to Max. She becomes hysterical, laughing and crying. She grabs the phone from Aaron.)*

MIRIAM. Maxele!?

MAX. Yes, my treasure, it's me.

MIRIAM. Oh, my darling, Max. I was so afraid that you were dead.

MAX. No, no my dear. Not yet.

MIRIAM. Oh, my darling, my darling, my darling … I'd rather die than leave you alone, *mein hartz, mein neshuma.* Where are you?

MAX. I've taken another name for myself — Dr. Sigmund Klein. I am at the Empire Hotel on Broadway. The eighth floor.

MIRIAM. I'll be right there. *(She hangs up. To Aaron:)* I am going to him now. Bring the baby to his mother. Come in the morning. *(She gathers her things, Aaron moves to kiss her … She runs out, leaving Aaron stunned.)*

AARON. *(To himself.)* She never made a secret of it — Max is her number one … until death. *(Lights change. Max's hotel room. Miriam hovers over a man who is barely recognizable.)*

MAX. Aaron! I must recite the "Blessed be He who restores the dead to life" over you. I was so worried when you did not come. *(Aaron approaches, bends down, and kisses him. Max takes Aaron's shoulders and kisses him.)*

AARON. Max — you told me not to c —

MAX. Ssssh. My friend, I am not well. But thank God I am not ready yet to give up the ghost.

AARON. Max, you'll be cured here. You'll be strong as an ox.

MIRIAM. Butterfly, don't let him become resigned. He'll come through this healthy and strong!

MAX. Nothing lasts forever. Arale, I sit here and think about those people whose last few dollars I took, and I want to die. *(He grabs Aaron's arm.)* I hope you told no one where I am. If they find out, they'll come flying like locusts and bury me alive. I know that Priva is moving heaven and earth to find me. And I am now penniless. I cannot pay for a doctor here to treat me. How long can it all go on?

AARON. Max, everything will end well, you will see.

MAX. Maybe it will, maybe it won't.

AARON. I'll find you money.

MAX. Suddenly the pauper is a banker. Look, Arale, if you and

Miriam are happy, I am happy. The truth is that I knew I would die soon ... and that is why I brought you two together. I lay there in the hospital in Warsaw, in agony, surrounded by drunks, degenerates, lunatics, and I had but one thought to comfort me; you two were in America and you loved each other. Since my own daughters perished, you are my children.

MIRIAM. Maxele, I am your wife, not your daughter. My place is with you.

MAX. Nonsense, I am approaching the end of my life while you are just beginning yours. My advice to you is this: Divorce that lunatic Stanley and marry Aaron. You are a fitting pair, truthless and luckless. *(He laughs, looking at the two of them. Aaron looks away.)*

MIRIAM. Max, you've become a matchmaker now?

MAX. Miriam, my darling, would you leave us for a moment? You have had not one hour of sleep, and I must speak to Aaron. *(Miriam looks at both men, upset. Then she kisses Max. She exits. Max settles in and looks at Aaron.)* Arale ... The whole idea of monogamy is a big lie. It was invented by women and by puritanical Christians. It never existed among Jews. Even our great teacher Moses craved a Nubian woman, and when his sister Miriam spoke ill of him she was struck with scabies. Where is it written that I must be saintlier than Moses or the patriarch Job? When a man is impotent he is dragged before the rabbi and forced to give his wife a divorce. But when a wife is frigid, cold as ice, she is praised for being chaste. My first wife, may she rest in peace, had that one redeeming virtue — so I was utterly miserable. But what of a woman who is born with hot blood? The whole world rises to condemn her. She is nothing but a whore. You know very well who I am talking about.

AARON. Miriam told you everything?

MAX. Everything.

AARON. You know her past?

MAX. Yes.

AARON. What would you call her then?

MAX. I would take her as she is.

AARON. Would you marry her?

MAX. If I were your age, yes.

AARON. But ... Max ...

MAX. *(He shakes his head.)* There is one thing I want you to promise me — don't deceive her.

AARON. I don't deceive her.

MAX. You do. You do. If you are not going to marry her, you must

tell her. She is pinning her hopes on you. What?! She's not like your mother — chaste, pure…? Aaron, as improbable as it may sound, when it comes to real love — what she feels for you — Miriam is a virtuous virgin. *(Music. Lights change. Days later. Miriam's apartment. Aaron, deep in thought, goes home.)*
MIRIAM. *(Calling to him.)* Arale, have you heard?
AARON. *(As he enters.)* Heard what?
MIRIAM. It's a miracle. Chaim Joel Treibitcher cabled Max that he has found a well-known doctor in Israel. He is offering to pay all Max's expenses and fly him there.
AARON. Really? But this is wonderful news. Chaim Joel is a generous and righteous man.
MIRIAM. *(Blunt.)* Aaron, I cannot remain in America as long as Max is in Israel. He is old; he requires my help and love. I want you to accompany me to Israel.
AARON. No, no I cannot go with the two of you. Really … *(Covering.)* Anyway, I am finally writing the first good book I have written in years.
MIRIAM. Ah! I know this. And what is this book about? Don't tell me. Does the corpse in "In the World of Chaos" finally come back to life?
AARON. Exactly so. It is about you.
MIRIAM. Not you?
AARON. *(He laughs.)* Well, yes. Of course. Me, too. We've both come back to life. *(She glows.)*
MIRIAM. Write it in Israel.
AARON. I cannot.
MIRIAM. Why won't you go?
AARON. You should be with Max. *(Miriam gets up. she pulls out a Bible.)* What are you doing?
MIRIAM. Be so good as to open the Bible to the Chapter of Curses for me. *(She hands him the Bible.)*
AARON. How do you know about the Chapter of Curses?
MIRIAM. I read about it in a story of yours. *(He opens the Bible to that chapter, Deut. 27-28.)*
AARON. These are sacred curses. No one but the most saintly of rabbis will read this aloud from the Torah for fear of being cursed. *(Miriam lights candles.)*
MIRIAM. *(Very quiet, over the candles.)* I swear by God in heaven and by the souls of those dear to me, the martyrs who perished at the hand of Hitler, may his name and his memory be obliterated,

that I shall have no other man in my life besides you. If I should break this sacred vow, may all the curses of the Holy Book descend on my head. *(Miriam reads the portion of curses.)* Cursed shall I be in the city and cursed shall I be in the country. The Lord shall set loose against me calamity, panic, and terror until I shall be utterly destroyed. The Lord will strike me with unknowable fear. I shall grope for my home, but I shall not live to find it. The Lord shall bring a nation against me which will swoop down like an eagle, a ruthless nation — that will show the old no regard and the young no mercy. I will be lost forever in lamentation because I would not serve the Lord my God. These are the terms of His covenant. Amen. *(She kisses the Bible and closes it.)*
AARON. Really, Miriam. How can you take such an oath?
MIRIAM. Whatever happens between us, I don't want you to lie awake at night thinking that I'm deceiving you with others.
AARON. What value does this oath have, coming from someone who does not believe in God?
MIRIAM. I believe in God.
AARON. This is new.
MIRIAM. ... Yes. *(Pause.)*
AARON. Shall I also take such an oath?
MIRIAM. No. You owe me nothing. I am going away from you, not you me. You may have whomever you please.
AARON. Tonight, you look like my mother when I was a small boy who went to *cheder* in Warsaw. You are like a newly married Hasidic bride and I your youthful ward. How can two candles costing pennies so alter the state of a man and a woman?
MIRIAM. Tonight I married you.
AARON. Miriam ...
MIRIAM. Don't worry. I won't force you into anything. I married you, not you me. I know that I am sinning gravely against God, against you, against Max. In the old days, I would have been ostracized or even stoned for it. *(She runs to him.)* Oh, Butterfly, it is so hard to leave you. I already miss you. I want to stay here with you, but Max is waiting for me. He is now my father. Do you understand? He is very ill. I am so frightened.
AARON. Of what are you frightened? *(Miriam does not answer.)*
MIRIAM. There is more to tell you ... *(She touches her fingers to Aaron's lips.)* Not tonight. *(She exits. Surreal light. Music. Aaron closes his eyes.)*
AARON. I dream it's Rosh Hashanah. My parents and I are all

going to *Tashlich* together, to throw our sins into the water to be washed away. The men lead the way. My father bends over my little brother, Moishe, speaking to him softly. The girls and the women appear, all decked out in their holiday finery. I see my mother. She wears the gold-colored dress she wore on her wedding day and which she always wears on the Days of Awe. Over her wig, a white silk shawl. "*Mameshi,* are you alive? I thought you died in Dzamboul, in Kazakhstan." Was there no war? Has the Messiah come? Has the resurrection of the dead begun? ... Miriam is near her. She's taking my mother's arm. We must be married. Yes! We're married! Oh, M*ameshi*, this is Miriam, your daughter-in-law, Miriam. *Mommelei,* you're alive! You're alive! *(Lights change. Sounds of airport in Israel. ("El Al Flight 883 has arrived from New York gate three. In Hebrew: El Al Flight 883 has arrived from New York ... " Aaron walks downstage. Miriam runs toward him. She kisses and embraces him, ecstatic.)*
MIRIAM. *(Breathless.)* Arale, you're here! You came ... *(They kiss and kiss.)*
AARON. How is Max?
MIRIAM. What can I say? Better. You will see him soon in Tel Aviv. Max won't stay in Jerusalem. He says it's too holy for him. *Meshugah* as ever, but also sweet. *(She starts to go. He stops her.)*
AARON. Look. *(They look out. Lights shift to a tiny surreal pool of light.)* Miriam ... We're here, in the Land of Israel, the land for which our ancestors yearned for two thousand years. *(Miriam: "yes.")* The sea is not some random body of water. It is *Yam Hagadol,* the Great Sea on which Jonah fled from God to be spared prophesying the destruction of Nineveh. *(Miriam: "Yes.")* Here sailed the merchant ships to which the Woman of Valor has been compared in the Book of Proverbs. *(Miriam: "Yes.")* Nearby Rachel still weeps over her children and refuses to be consoled. *(Miriam gets tears in her eyes, squeezes his hand. Miriam: "Yes ... ")* — It is fitting to be in Israel for the first time ... with you ... *(They kiss.)*
MIRIAM. *(Putting her arm through his.)* I have a surprise for you. Chaim Joel is throwing you a party.
AARON. A party? ... I am not going.
MIRIAM. But why? You must go! We cannot miss another of Chaim Joel's parties.
AARON. I don't do well with lots of people. One person, even two or three I can easily tolerate, but an assemblage of people strikes me with fear. Mobs launch wars, inquisitions, expulsions —
MIRIAM. Oh, stop. This is not a mob. This is a party thrown in

your honor. You are going to be presented with a literary prize.
AARON. A prize?
MIRIAM. Yes, Chaim Joel has set up an award for five hundred dollars in Matilda's name!
AARON. Well. That's nice. *(Miriam laughs. She takes his hand.)*
MIRIAM. Butterfly, I have lacked the courage to speak with you about something very important. While I have been here, nursing Max, I have had time to think. I am approaching thirty, and I would like to have a child before I lie dead in my grave. Why did I survive the war if not to produce someone who will be worthy of the name "man"? To what end is all our love and all our passion …
AARON. What will you do if I tell you we will not have a child, look for another father?
MIRIAM. No. I will never break my vow to you. *(Pause.)* There's no need to answer me now.
AARON. We will have a child. I want a child. Our child. *(Miriam looks at him as if ready to laugh and cry at the same time. Lights change. Celebratory Jewish music. Party sounds. The party. Decorations. Max enters. He is very ill but tries to be hearty, tries to dance if only with his arms. Max calls out to Aaron.)*
MAX. Aaron! Why are you hiding yourself like a shy bride? *(They laugh.)* You are, after all, the guest of honor tonight. Come, come on, you two. There is a feast inside and dancing. We are all waiting for you.
AARON. Coming, coming … *(As he approaches them.)* Can you believe it, Max? *(Laughing and happy.)* For the first time in my life, I am experiencing a taste of fame, and do you know what? I think I *like* it! *(Miriam laughs. Aaron turns to her. With tears in his eyes.)* This is the happiest night of *my* life.
MIRIAM. Oh, Arale … *(She throws her arms around him.)*
MAX. Author! Author! Come … I want to introduce you to everyone! *(As Aaron, Miriam, and Max move towards the dinner, a woman stops Aaron. Her eyes are black. Even before she opens her mouth, Aaron knows she is from Poland and a victim of Hitler.)*
WOMAN. Mr. Greidinger … Forgive me for disturbing you. I am a reader of yours. I must speak to you about a certain matter. Can we talk? It is urgent.
AARON. Yes, certainly. *(To Max and Miriam.)* You two go in. I'll be with you in a moment. *(As Aaron finds a secluded corner:)*
WOMAN. The matter I want to discuss with you is very, very important. I hesitated all evening whether or not to approach you.

My daughter attended the Gymnasium in Warsaw with Miriam Zalkind. My daughter, unfortunately, is no longer among the living. Miriam does not recognize me now — how could she? At that time I was relatively young, but now I am neither young nor well.
AARON. What is your name? Miriam will be glad to hear about you.
WOMAN. I don't want Miriam to hear about me. I beg you, don't be angry with me. What I want to tell you will not be pleasant for you to hear, but I feel it is my duty to speak to an honored Jewish writer.
AARON. Yes, I understand, but I want you to know that we cannot judge those who have been the victims of Hitler ... I mean, I cannot judge. You are probably —
WOMAN. Yes, I lived through that hell, all of it.
AARON. So did Miriam.
WOMAN. ... What the murderers did to us, that God will judge someday. But those who helped the murderers and served them — for them I have nothing but contempt.
AARON. What do you mean?
WOMAN. You must hear me out. Don't worry. I am not about to tell you all I endured at the hands of the Nazis ... I want you to know that what I am doing now I do with a heavy heart. *(She takes a deep breath.)* At the end of 1944, we were dragged with hundreds of other lost souls by freighter to Stutthof ... It was clear that the Nazis had lost the war, but whether we would live to see our liberation was an open question. Now comes the part I feel compelled to tell you: Miriam was in Stutthof.
AARON. No, no. I am afraid you are mistaken —
WOMAN. I saw her as clearly as I see you now. Miriam was one of their *kapos*.
AARON. W — *kapos*...! What do you mean?
WOMAN. What do I mean? She worked for them. She was the mistress of the SS officer Wolfgang Schmidt. I believe you know that a Jewish girl did not become a *kapo* for her good deeds. Some *kapos* thrashed Jewish girls for the smallest sins, for being slow when called for work, for trying to steal a potato. Some even helped the Nazis take children to the gas chambers. Well, that's what I wanted to tell you. *(Silence.)*
AARON. Are you sure that it was she?
WOMAN. She used to visit our home. I'd recognize her a mile away. *(Silence.)*
AARON. *(Barely able to speak.)* I've heard among the *kapos* there

were some decent people ... who helped the inmates. *(Woman turns away in contempt.)* Do you know what Miriam did? Do you know ... if she helped — ? *(The woman shrugs.)*

WOMAN. I told you what I know. *(Miriam enters. The woman sees her. Pale, unsteady, she opens her mouth to speak but utters not a sound.)*

MIRIAM. Arale, where have you been all this time? I've been looking for you.

WOMAN. *(Voice breaking.)* I'm leaving. Good night, *mein kind*.

AARON. Yes, good night, and again — thank you. *(The woman leaves.)*

MIRIAM. Who was that woman? What did she want?

AARON. *(Mouth dry.)* A teacher. She needed some advice.

MIRIAM. You're dispensing advice here, too? *(She looks again after her.)* Tell me, what did that woman want? She looks familiar to me.

AARON. Let's go. *(He takes her hand.)*

MIRIAM. Ah! Your hand is so cold!

AARON. Which way do we go? *(He turns and suddenly collapses, faint.)*

MIRIAM. Aaron! *(She kneels at his side.)*

AARON. I'm cold.

MIRIAM. I'll get you something. *(Miriam runs to get help.)*

AARON. Ah, so this is what hell must be ... *(Miriam returns with a blanket and fusses over him like a devoted wife.)*

MIRIAM. Are you still cold? *(Aaron nods. She tucks the blanket around him. He throws it off.)*

AARON. No, I am hot. Get me some ice, some water. *(She runs to go.)* Oh, my God, Miriam! *(She stops, looks at him, terrified.)*

MIRIAM. I am going to get a doctor ... *(Desperate.)* Who was that woman? *(He will not answer. Terrified, she exits.)*

AARON. *(Muttering.)* Dear God ... she wanted to *live*. I can hear my mother say, "Better she should have died." *(Lights change. Music. Lights up on Max in a wheelchair. Miriam wheels him in. Aaron stands by, uncomfortable. The next morning.)*

MAX. He is leaving? Why?

MIRIAM. Maxele, he has his work.

MAX. I am destined to die soon, I want to be buried in this ancient soil. And you, Arale, you want to leave it.

AARON. *(Lying.)* My editor says I must come right back to New York.

MAX. Of course. Well ... Come back to us, Arale. Promise me you will come back; I want to see you one more time. I don't want

to die without you. You two are my children.
MIRIAM. Shhhhh ... Max ...
AARON. Max, I will see you. *(Miriam takes Max's hand. Aaron kisses him.)*
MAX. Ah! Now ... maybe a breath of life remains. I think I feel it.
MIRIAM. *(To Aaron.)* I'll come to New York later. *(Aaron will not look at her. To Max.)* We'll all go back to America, and soon.
MAX. Ach ... I wish I could dance at your wedding. Every marriage, Aaron, is an act of *tikkun*. You won't believe me saying this but it's true, even though our rebbe used to say it. Every good marriage helps mend the world. *(To Aaron with great love.)* So ... She brought you back to life; take care of her after I'm dead. *(Aaron brushes tears out of his eyes, kisses Max, looks at Miriam, agonized, turns to go. Worried.)* Arale? *(Aaron turns to Max. He does not answer.)* Arale? *(Aaron takes Miriam aside as if to kiss her. Instead he takes her face in his hands so Max cannot hear:)*
AARON. I know everything.
MIRIAM. *(A gasp, agonized.)* Ah! No ... *(Pause.)* There was so much more I would tell you. *(She reaches for him.)*
AARON. No. Don't ... please ... *(Lights change. Aaron walks downstage. Stops.)* ... I feel like an old man. I've lived through two world wars ... My entire family has perished ... I no longer live as my forebears lived. I've severed myself from the root ... I am a remnant of a spiritual holocaust ... And Miriam ... I went to Israel thinking of her as my bride. And now? All I can think about is the woman who told me ... a *kapo* ... I can hardly believe it. Yet I have the peculiar feeling that I have seen and heard all this before, either while awake or in a dream. The figure of Wolfgang Schmidt floats before my eyes. I hear him shouting at Miriam in a rasping voice. My heart breaks for her. *(In the shadows, the figure of Miriam slowly emerges. She holds a cable out to him. Music begins, a haunting* nigun, *full of sorrow. Miriam's voice, almost a whisper:)*
MIRIAM. "Please, Aaron. I hope you read this cable, even though it's from me. Max died tonight in his sleep."
AARON. Max died...? Ah ...
MIRIAM. "Forgive me, Aaron. Your Miriam." *(Lights out on Miriam.)*
AARON. My Miriam ... It is true ... *My* Miriam. I cannot live without her. *(Miriam enters. Music continues. She walks slowly toward him. He looks at her. They look at each other a long time.)*
MIRIAM. *(Simply.)* Arale, I love you. *(Pause.)*

AARON. And I you.
MIRIAM. *(Tentative, deeply sad.)* Butterfly, if we are fortunate enough to have a son … perhaps we should name him Max … *(Long pause.)*
AARON. *(Agonized.)* Miriam … You know there can be no children.
MIRIAM. No children, but why? *(This is very difficult for Aaron to say. He struggles with himself.)*
AARON. For some, marriage is an investment in the future. For us, it is about the past. What we know should not be passed down. We must be like mules. The last of a generation. *(Aaron offers Miriam his hand. After a long time, she takes it. They embrace. Music fades out.)*

End of Play

PROPERTY LIST

Sheaf of letters (AARON)
Cigar (MAX)
Coffee (WAITER, MIRIAM)
Pill box and pills (MAX)
Small, heart-shaped box of chocolates (MAX)
Phone (AARON, MIRIAM, AARON)
Fruit, rolls, breakfast food (AARON)
Pen and paper (AARON)
Revolver (STANLEY)
Cigarette (MIRIAM)
Bag with belongings — money, keys, checkbook (MIRIAM)
Dime (AARON)
Baby (MIRIAM)
Newspaper — *Yiddish Forward* (MIRIAM)
Bible (MIRIAM)
Candles, matches (MIRIAM)
Blanket (MIRIAM)
Telegram (MIRIAM)

SOUND EFFECTS

Street noise
Music
Phone ringing
Voice-over (MAX)
Sounds of Israeli airport
Voice-overs in English and Hebrew
Jewish celebratory music, party sounds

NEW PLAYS

★ **MONTHS ON END by Craig Pospisil.** In comic scenes, one for each month of the year, we follow the intertwined worlds of a circle of friends and family whose lives are poised between happiness and heartbreak. "...a triumph...these twelve vignettes all form crucial pieces in the eternal puzzle known as human relationships, an area in which the playwright displays an assured knowledge that spans deep sorrow to unbounded happiness." –*Ann Arbor News*. "...rings with emotional truth, humor...[an] endearing contemplation on love...entertaining and satisfying." –*Oakland Press*. [5M, 5W] ISBN: 0-8222-1892-5

★ **GOOD THING by Jessica Goldberg.** Brings us into the households of John and Nancy Roy, forty-something high-school guidance counselors whose marriage has been increasingly on the rocks and Dean and Mary, recent graduates struggling to make their way in life. "...a blend of gritty social drama, poetic humor and unsubtle existential contemplation..." –*Variety*. [3M, 3W] ISBN: 0-8222-1869-0

★ **THE DEAD EYE BOY by Angus MacLachlan.** Having fallen in love at their Narcotics Anonymous meeting, Billy and Shirley-Diane are striving to overcome the past together. But their relationship is complicated by the presence of Sorin, Shirley-Diane's fourteen-year-old son, a damaged reminder of her dark past. "...a grim, insightful portrait of an unmoored family..." –*NY Times*. "MacLachlan's play isn't for the squeamish, but then, tragic stories delivered at such an unrelenting fever pitch rarely are." –*Variety*. [1M, 1W, 1 boy] ISBN: 0-8222-1844-5

★ **[SIC] by Melissa James Gibson.** In adjacent apartments three young, ambitious neighbors come together to discuss, flirt, argue, share their dreams and plan their futures with unequal degrees of deep hopefulness and abject despair. "A work...concerned with the sound and power of language..." –*NY Times*. "...a wonderfully original take on urban friendship and the comedy of manners—a *Design for Living* for our times..." –*NY Observer*. [3M, 2W] ISBN: 0-8222-1872-0

★ **LOOKING FOR NORMAL by Jane Anderson.** Roy and Irma's twenty-five-year marriage is thrown into turmoil when Roy confesses that he is actually a woman trapped in a man's body, forcing the couple to wrestle with the meaning of their marriage and the delicate dynamics of family. "Jane Anderson's bittersweet transgender domestic comedy-drama …is thoughtful and touching and full of wit and wisdom. A real audience pleaser." –*Hollywood Reporter*. [5M, 4W] ISBN: 0-8222-1857-7

★ **ENDPAPERS by Thomas McCormack.** The regal Joshua Maynard, the old and ailing head of a mid-sized, family-owned book-publishing house in New York City, must name a successor. One faction in the house backs a smart, "pragmatic" manager, the other faction a smart, "sensitive" editor and both factions fear what the other's man could do to this house— and to them. "If Kaufman and Hart had undertaken a comedy about the publishing business, they might have written *Endpapers*...a breathlessly fast, funny, and thoughtful comedy …keeps you amused, guessing, and often surprised...profound in its empathy for the paradoxes of human nature." –*NY Magazine*. [7M, 4W] ISBN: 0-8222-1908-5

★ **THE PAVILION by Craig Wright.** By turns poetic and comic, romantic and philosophical, this play asks old lovers to face the consequences of difficult choices made long ago. "The script's greatest strength lies in the genuineness of its feeling." –*Houston Chronicle*. "Wright's perceptive, gently witty writing makes this familiar situation fresh and thoroughly involving." –*Philadelphia Inquirer*. [2M, 1W (flexible casting)] ISBN: 0-8222-1898-4

DRAMATISTS PLAY SERVICE, INC.
440 Park Avenue South, New York, NY 10016 212-683-8960 Fax 212-213-1539
postmaster@dramatists.com   www.dramatists.com

NEW PLAYS

★ **BE AGGRESSIVE by Annie Weisman.** Vista Del Sol is paradise, sandy beaches, avocado-lined streets. But for seventeen-year-old cheerleader Laura, everything changes when her mother is killed in a car crash, and she embarks on a journey to the Spirit Institute of the South where she can learn "cheer" with Bible belt intensity. "...filled with lingual gymnastics...stylized rapid-fire dialogue..." –*Variety*. "...a new, exciting, and unique voice in the American theatre..." –*BackStage West*. [1M, 4W, extras] ISBN: 0-8222-1894-1

★ **FOUR by Christopher Shinn.** Four people struggle desperately to connect in this quiet, sophisticated, moving drama. "...smart, broken-hearted...Mr. Shinn has a precocious and forgiving sense of how power shifts in the game of sexual pursuit...He promises to be a playwright to reckon with..." –*NY Times*. "A voice emerges from an American place. It's got humor, sadness and a fresh and touching rhythm that tell of the loneliness and secrets of life...[a] poetic, haunting play." –*NY Post*. [3M, 1W] ISBN: 0-8222-1850-X

★ **WONDER OF THE WORLD by David Lindsay-Abaire.** A madcap picaresque involving Niagara Falls, a lonely tour-boat captain, a pair of bickering private detectives and a husband's dirty little secret. "Exceedingly whimsical and playfully wicked. Winning and genial. A top-drawer production." –*NY Times*. "Full frontal lunacy is on display. A most assuredly fresh and hilarious tragicomedy of marital discord run amok...absolutely hysterical..." –*Variety*. [3M, 4W (doubling)] ISBN: 0-8222-1863-1

★ **QED by Peter Parnell.** Nobel Prize-winning physicist and all-around genius Richard Feynman holds forth with captivating wit and wisdom in this fascinating biographical play that originally starred Alan Alda. "QED is a seductive mix of science, human affections, moral courage, and comic eccentricity. It reflects on, among other things, death, the absence of God, travel to an unexplored country, the pleasures of drumming, and the need to know and understand." –*NY Magazine*. "Its rhythms correspond to the way that people—even geniuses—approach and avoid highly emotional issues, and it portrays Feynman with affection and awe." –*The New Yorker*. [1M, 1W] ISBN: 0-8222-1924-7

★ **UNWRAP YOUR CANDY by Doug Wright.** Alternately chilling and hilarious, this deliciously macabre collection of four bedtime tales for adults is guaranteed to keep you awake for nights on end. "Engaging and intellectually satisfying...a treat to watch." –*NY Times*. "Fiendishly clever. Mordantly funny and chilling. Doug Wright teases, freezes and zaps us." –*Village Voice*. "Four bite-size plays that bite back." –*Variety*. [flexible casting] ISBN: 0-8222-1871-2

★ **FURTHER THAN THE FURTHEST THING by Zinnie Harris.** On a remote island in the middle of the Atlantic secrets are buried. When the outside world comes calling, the islanders find their world blown apart from the inside as well as beyond. "Harris winningly produces an intimate and poetic, as well as political, family saga." –*Independent (London)*. "Harris' enthralling adventure of a play marks a departure from stale, well-furrowed theatrical terrain." –*Evening Standard (London)*. [3M, 2W] ISBN: 0-8222-1874-7

★ **THE DESIGNATED MOURNER by Wallace Shawn.** The story of three people living in a country where what sort of books people like to read and how they choose to amuse themselves becomes both firmly personal and unexpectedly entangled with questions of survival. "This is a playwright who does not just tell you what it is like to be arrested at night by goons or to fall morally apart and become an aimless yet weirdly contented ghost yourself. He has the originality to make you feel it." –*Times (London)*. "A fascinating play with beautiful passages of writing..." –*Variety*. [2M, 1W] ISBN: 0-8222-1848-8

DRAMATISTS PLAY SERVICE, INC.
440 Park Avenue South, New York, NY 10016 212-683-8960 Fax 212-213-1539
postmaster@dramatists.com www.dramatists.com

NEW PLAYS

★ **SHEL'S SHORTS by Shel Silverstein.** Lauded poet, songwriter and author of children's books, the incomparable Shel Silverstein's short plays are deeply infused with the same wicked sense of humor that made him famous. "…[a] childlike honesty and twisted sense of humor." *–Boston Herald.* "…terse dialogue and an absurdity laced with a tang of dread give [*Shel's Shorts*] more than a trace of Samuel Beckett's comic existentialism." *–Boston Phoenix.* [flexible casting] ISBN: 0-8222-1897-6

★ **AN ADULT EVENING OF SHEL SILVERSTEIN by Shel Silverstein.** Welcome to the darkly comic world of Shel Silverstein, a world where nothing is as it seems and where the most innocent conversation can turn menacing in an instant. These ten imaginative plays vary widely in content, but the style is unmistakable. "…[*An Adult Evening*] shows off Silverstein's virtuosic gift for wordplay…[and] sends the audience out…with a clear appreciation of human nature as perverse and laughable." *–NY Times.* [flexible casting] ISBN: 0-8222-1873-9

★ **WHERE'S MY MONEY? by John Patrick Shanley.** A caustic and sardonic vivisection of the institution of marriage, laced with the author's inimitable razor-sharp wit. "…Shanley's gift for acid-laced one-liners and emotionally tumescent exchanges is certainly potent…" *–Variety.* "…lively, smart, occasionally scary and rich in reverse wisdom." *–NY Times.* [3M, 3W] ISBN: 0-8222-1865-8

★ **A FEW STOUT INDIVIDUALS by John Guare.** A wonderfully screwy comedy-drama that figures Ulysses S. Grant in the throes of writing his memoirs, surrounded by a cast of fantastical characters, including the Emperor and Empress of Japan, the opera star Adelina Patti and Mark Twain. "Guare's smarts, passion and creativity skyrocket to awesome heights…" *–Star Ledger.* "…precisely the kind of good new play that you might call an everyday miracle…every minute of it is fresh and newly alive…" *–Village Voice.* [10M, 3W] ISBN: 0-8222-1907-7

★ **BREATH, BOOM by Kia Corthron.** A look at fourteen years in the life of Prix, a Bronx native, from her ruthless girl-gang leadership at sixteen through her coming to maturity at thirty. "…vivid world, believable and eye-opening, a place worthy of a dramatic visit, where no one would want to live but many have to." *–NY Times.* "…rich with humor, terse vernacular strength and gritty detail…" *–Variety.* [1M, 9W] ISBN: 0-8222-1849-6

★ **THE LATE HENRY MOSS by Sam Shepard.** Two antagonistic brothers, Ray and Earl, are brought together after their father, Henry Moss, is found dead in his seedy New Mexico home in this classic Shepard tale. "…His singular gift has been for building mysteries out of the ordinary ingredients of American family life…" *–NY Times.* "…rich moments …Shepard finds gold." *–LA Times.* [7M, 1W] ISBN: 0-8222-1858-5

★ **THE CARPETBAGGER'S CHILDREN by Horton Foote.** One family's history spanning from the Civil War to WWII is recounted by three sisters in evocative, intertwining monologues. "…bittersweet music—[a] rhapsody of ambivalence…in its modest, garrulous way…theatrically daring." *–The New Yorker.* [3W] ISBN: 0-8222-1843-7

★ **THE NINA VARIATIONS by Steven Dietz.** In this funny, fierce and heartbreaking homage to *The Seagull*, Dietz puts Chekhov's star-crossed lovers in a room and doesn't let them out. "A perfect little jewel of a play…" *–Shepherdstown Chronicle.* "…a delightful revelation of a writer at play; and also an odd, haunting, moving theater piece of lingering beauty." *–Eastside Journal (Seattle).* [1M, 1W (flexible casting)] ISBN: 0-8222-1891-7

DRAMATISTS PLAY SERVICE, INC.
440 Park Avenue South, New York, NY 10016 212-683-8960 Fax 212-213-1539
postmaster@dramatists.com   www.dramatists.com